Dear Parent:
Your child's love of reading starts here!

Every child learns to read in a different way and at his or her own speed. Some go back and forth between reading levels and read favorite books again and again. Others read through each level in order. You can help your young reader improve and become more confident by encouraging his or her own interests and abilities. From books your child reads with you to the first books he or she reads alone, there are I Can Read Books for every stage of reading:

SHARED READING
Basic language, word repetition, and whimsical illustrations, ideal for sharing with your emergent reader

BEGINNING READING
Short sentences, familiar words, and simple concepts for children eager to read on their own

READING WITH HELP
Engaging stories, longer sentences, and language play for developing readers

READING ALONE
Complex plots, challenging vocabulary, and high-interest topics for the independent reader

ADVANCED READING
Short paragraphs, chapters, and exciting themes for the perfect bridge to chapter books

I Can Read Books have introduced children to the joy of reading since 1957. Featuring award-winning authors and illustrators and a fabulous cast of beloved characters, I Can Read Books set the standard for beginning readers.

A lifetime of discovery begins with the magical words **"I Can Read!"**

*Visit www.icanread.com for information
on enriching your child's reading experience.*

I Can Read Book® is a trademark of HarperCollins Publishers.

Pete the Cat and the Surprise Teacher. Copyright © 2017 by James Dean. All rights reserved. Printed in the United States of America. No part of this book may be used or reproduced in any manner whatsoever without written permission except in the case of brief quotations embodied in critical articles and reviews. For information address HarperCollins Children's Books, a division of HarperCollins Publishers, 195 Broadway, New York, NY 10007.
www.icanread.com

Library of Congress Control Number: 2016906657
ISBN 978-0-06-240429-9 (trade bdg.) — ISBN 978-0-06-240428-2 (pbk.)

18 19 20 LSCC 10 9 8 7 6 5   ❖   First Edition

Pete the Cat

AND THE SURPRISE TEACHER

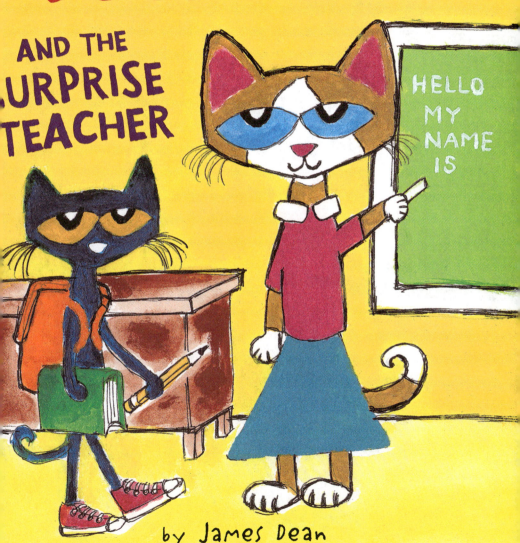

HELLO
MY
NAME
IS

by James Dean

HARPER
An Imprint of HarperCollinsPublishers

Pete is ready for school.
"Where is Mom?" Pete asks.

"She has a surprise for you,"
says Pete's dad.

Pete goes to school.

His mom is there.

What a surprise!

"Hi, class. I am Mrs. Cat,"
says Pete's mom.
"I am the substitute teacher."

"I will need your help today,"
says Pete's mom.
"What do we do first?"

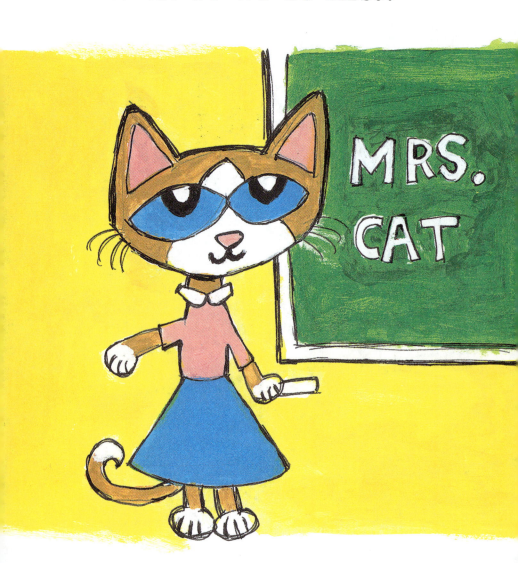

"Art!" says Pete.

"Yeah!" says the class.

The class lines up.

Pete's mom leads the line.

"Is this art?" asks Pete's mom.

Boing!

This is not art.

This is gym.

"Stay and play!"

says the gym teacher.

The class plays.

"Gym is fun with more kids!"

says Pete.

Gym is over.
Pete's mom takes
the class to art.

La, la, la!

This is not art.

This is music.

"Stay and sing!"

says the music teacher.

The class sings.
"We are louder with
more kids!" says Pete.

Rumble!

Pete is hungry.

Time for lunch!

This is not the
lunchroom.

This is the playground!
"Let's have a picnic,"
says Pete.

"Now it is time
for art," says Pete's mom.
Everyone cheers.

Pete leads the class.

"Is this art?"

asks Pete's mom.

It is!

Lots of kids are

making art.

"Oh no," says the art teacher.
"It is too late to join us.
The day is almost over."

The class goes to
their classroom.
"I know!" says Pete.

"Let's make art here!"
he says.
"Okay," says Pete's mom.

Pete calls a huddle.

Whisper, whisper.

The class plans a surprise.

Pete draws.

Callie makes paper cats.

Everyone helps.

"Surprise!" says Pete.
The class made art for
Pete's mom!

"Thank you, Mrs. Cat!"
says the class. "We had a
great day with you!"

Sometimes a different day
is an awesome day!